LETTS GUIDES TO
✧ GARDEN DESIGN ✧
Small Garden

LETTS GUIDES TO
✧ GARDEN DESIGN ✧

Small
Garden

✧ ROGER GROUNDS ✧

CANOPY BOOKS
A Division of Abbeville Publishing Group
NEW YORK LONDON PARIS

First published in the United States in 1994
by Canopy Books, a division of Abbeville Publishing Group
488 Madison Avenue
New York NY 10022

First published in the United Kingdom in 1993
by Charles Letts & Co Ltd.
Letts of London House, Parkgate Road
London SW11 4NQ

Series editor: Diana Saville

Edited, designed and produced by Robert Ditchfield Ltd.
Copyright © Robert Ditchfield Ltd. 1993.

ISBN 1-55859-661-5

A CIP catalogue record for this book is available from the British Library.

ACKNOWLEDGMENTS

Photographs are reproduced by kind permission of the following: Robert Ditchfield
Ltd.: 12, 13, 14, 15, 26, 33 (York Gate, photographer Jerry Hardman-Jones); Roger
Grounds: 18, 25 (The Little Cottage, Lymington); Jerry Harpur: cover (designer
Thomasina Tarling, Chelsea); Andrew Lawson: 2, 6, 8 (designer Anthea Gibson), 9,
19 (sculptor Bryony Lawson), 30, 31; W. A. Lord: 17, 21, 22, 24, 36 (Denmans), 55
(Arley Hall); S & O Matthews: 10, 24, 25, 39, 44, 53; Clive Nichols: 11, 28 (both
Fulham garden, designer Anthony Noel), 20; Christine Skelmersdale: 49. All other
photographs are by Diana Saville who would like to thank the owners of the
gardens which include: Appleshaw garden 16; Bourton House 26/27; Close Farm
38, 40; Docwra's Manor 41; Edenbridge House 42/43; Hergest Croft 29; Kiftsgate 52;
Powis Castle 1; Preen Manor 5, 43 below, 45; Sissinghurst 35; Snowshill 32;
Stone Cottage 34; Woodpeckers 17, 48, 49.

ILLUSTRATIONS

Page 1: Hamamelis mollis over golden carex and gold-variegated ivy.
Frontispiece: A chaenomeles and bergenia harmonize gracefully.
Page 5: Small formal water garden with trimmed box in tubs.

CONTENTS

LEFT: *The structure of a garden is thrown into relief by snow.*

OPPOSITE: *The white garden at Sissinghurst is rigidly disciplined, though the planting is relaxed.*

the more inescapable its problems and the more helpful the solutions offered by design and the skilled use of plants.

Good design is more than merely a matter of solving problems: it aims to make of a garden a thing of beauty, a place in which to rest the mind and delight the senses.

We tend to think of gardens primarily in terms of flowers. But flowers are relative newcomers to our gardens, and until a hundred years or so ago gardens in the West were composed of trees and grass and gravel and water, with a few stone ornaments. It is still possible to create highly satisfying gardens using only these elements. The flowers when they came, were imposed on this pre-existent framework. We still perceive gardens in this historical perspective and still design the framework before furnishing it with plants and flowers.

In order to create a satisfying ornamental garden it is first necessary, while bearing constantly in mind the colours and flowers one is likely to use, to remove them from the inner eye and to concentrate the mind on the structure or framework of the garden.

INTRODUCTION

The art of gardening is to make the most of those plants that have particular likings for particular places. Design offers the means of achieving desired effects.

The purpose of designing a garden is to ensure that the finished effect is finer than it would have been had the garden come about by chance. The smaller a garden

6

A tiny, elegant city garden is organized by repeated vertical lines and trelliswork.

STRUCTURE

The art of designing the framework of a garden is to perceive in high summer how the garden will look in winter, stripped of its beguiling flowers, for winter is the acid test of a garden, when the strength of its structure is revealed. This is most telling not when the structure is thrown into high drama by the chiaroscuro of snow and low light, nor by the meretricious glitter of frost, but on a sunless, sodden mid-winter day. Even on such a day a well-de-

signed garden will invite the eye to explore its spatial relationships. This is more intensely true of a small garden than a larger one, for a small garden is likely to be revealed in its entirety, and seeing it may be unavoidable.

What makes a small garden feel good in winter is the way its space is used. This is determined firstly but only partly by its boundaries. More important is the ground plan – the pattern made by paths, beds and borders, lawns and the spaces between these. Just as important are the vertical elements, hedges, walls and fences, the shapes of the trees and the shadows they cast.

Garden design, reduced to

its most abstract, is concerned with organizing space and manipulating light. Its sense of space is determined by its boundaries and its internal divisions: light is manipulated in terms of colour and distance. Seen in these terms, garden making is about rhythm, pattern and repetition.

The division of space is crucial. In the French classical gardens a rigid, systematic series of spaces is imposed on the ground plan, using trees, bosquets and box edging (Vaux le Vicomte, Versailles). The Moorish tradition relies on columns or colonnades to divide space (The Alhambra) and this allows volume and void to mix and mingle in a manner impossible in a French garden. A lime walk, an orchard and even, to a lesser degree, a woodland garden, rely on this method. The English landscape garden relies on an alternation of volume and void – the bulk of tree groups balanced against the void of close-cropped grass (Petworth, Stowe). To the casual eye, in an informal garden space may not seem to be defined at all: proportion in fact is vital.

The finest English gardens (Hidcote, Sissinghurst) combine two traditions of space division, the French formal and the English landscape, the structure rigidly disciplined as in the French, the planting loose and organic as in the English landscape, but reduced to shrubs and perennials, both interweaving to create a sense of motion, thereby becoming a more stimulating style than either would be on its own.

The Art of Stretching

The mirror, invisibly placed within the white arches, doubles the length of the garden.

Gardens are almost by definition enclosed. The general desire is to make gardens seem larger than they are. The conventional wisdom is that this is best achieved firstly by obscuring and softening the boundaries with plants, and secondly by so dividing the garden with shrubs or trellis that it cannot be seen in its entirety at a single glance. This is essentially the method of the English landscape garden school, and it was first applied to relatively small, enclosed town gardens by the poet Alexander Pope, who laid out his villa at Twickenham in this way. Its limitation is that it presupposes that a garden is a picture to be viewed, probably from the main rooms of the house.

But there is another tradition. The earliest ornamental gardens were probably Persian, predating classical antiquity. Typically they were courtyards enclosed on all four sides by the house whose rooms opened directly into the garden. A colonnaded peristyle ran round the courtyard, enabling one to get from one room to another under cover in wet weather.

9

LEFT: *The formal boundary hedge to the front of the garden defines the style; though architectural, its topiary topping suits the cottage.*

is created that something lies beyond, another compartment, perhaps, full of the soft greenness of ferns or grasses. This compartment need be no more than a metre deep.

In larger, rectangular gardens two approximately equal compartments are preferable, the one nearest the house based on the concept of a room, the other on the concept of a landscape park, each gaining from the other. Long, thin gardens are best treated as a developing sequence.

In such an arrangement the garden is seen as another room, an oasis of green surrounding a central pool and fountain, each room having its own distinct purpose, the kitchen for cooking, the bedroom for sleeping. The purpose of the garden was to refresh the senses, all of them.

Such a treatment is often appropriate in small, especially town, gardens.

Boundaries

In a small garden every treatment from a boudoir to a landscaped park is possible, so long as it is appreciated that it is the boundaries that set the tone. This is because anything that is vertical, such as a wall or fence, presents itself very strongly to the eye. Ground surface, by contrast, is of secondary importance.

The most intimate rooms are most readily created in small, walled town gardens. The walls may be left plain or may be painted, either in flat colours or decorated with a pattern of panels. In antiquity the panels might have contained paintings of nymphs and shepherds. *Trompe l'oeil* effects can enchant: an open window giving onto parkland, or a real window fixed to the wall with mirrors where the glass should be, which when opened reveals a vista to the sea. Or *trompe l'oeil* trellis can be used to create the illusion of a statue at the end of a corridor. Trellis can be used to create the illusion of walls. White trellis in front of darker walls or fences is most effective.

The intimacy of a garden is intensified if the illusion

Planting Boundaries

The style of a garden can as readily be created by the way the boundaries are planted as by artefacts. Formal planting such as hedges, will reinforce the four-squareness of an enclosure. Informal planting that breaks up the boundary will lessen the sense of enclosure. Intermediates are possible.

The best hedges are made from box and yew, beech and hornbeam. Box and yew are treasured for the dark glossiness of their evergreen leaves, the deciduous beech and hornbeam for their fresh green in spring, and foxy redness in winter. Where yew is too dark or too slow, hemlock (*Tsuga heterophylla*) may be better. The very darkness of yew can be exploited in two-compart-

RIGHT: Trompe l'oeil *trellis* *gives the effect of a recess,* *pushing the wall back from* *the planted pot.*

ment gardens, where it can be used to enhance the nearness of the first compartment, while greys are used to create distance in the second.

Where boundaries are not tall enough to ensure privacy, stilt hedges will give extra height, the stilts themselves breaking up space into interesting intervals. Stilt hedges are made by planting young feathered standards one or two metres apart, initially training the upper branches along horizontal wires stretched between poles, rubbing off the lower buds and branches and later trimming the upper branches like an ordinary hedge. Beech or hornbeam are best. Another option is a double hedge, where the space beneath a stilt hedge is filled with an underplanting of box, and both are trimmed in the same vertical plane. This creates a light green/dark green effect in summer, foxy-red/dark green in winter.

The harsh straight lines along the top of a wall, hedge or fence can less formally be broken up by colonnades, which at their simplest may be stripped poles with swags of rope slung between them, and covered with climbing roses or wisteria, and late summer- to autumn-flowering clematis (*C. viticella* and its forms). This also breaks up the length of the boundary, dividing it into regular intervals. Repetition along an axis impels the eye forward, and makes the distance covered seem greater than it is. Such rhythm and repetition also tends to create a sense of ease and harmony.

Boundaries may be totally clothed with climbers, specially where space is at a premium, or concealed behind a dense boskage of shrubs and trees. Such plantings are most pleasing when some sense of rhythm, pattern and repetition is built into the scheme, where for example the same plant is repeated at approximately equal intervals, or where every third or fourth plant is an evergreen, not necessarily the same one. Generally not more than one third of the plants in a garden should be evergreen, but in town gardens the proportion may be higher, especially if the foliage is varied. Trees are generally planted against the boundary, the shrubs further in. But if the trees are planted at the front of the border, and the shrubs against the boundary, an even greater sense of space may be created, especially as the stems of the trees will create a sense of vertical space, and may be used to reinforce the sense of rhythm.

11

LEFT: *Ground level interest in the form of diamond-patterned paths (formed of setts) meeting at a circle.*

OPPOSITE: *A sunken garden reached by curving steps lures the eye down.*

GROUND SURFACE AND AREA

If you walk into a garden which strikes you at once as happy and harmonious, this is more often than not because of the way the space on the ground has been used. Ground space is divided by changes in texture or level, and the key to harmony is the Golden Mean, which is more than merely a ratio: it has correspondences in the inner mind. Thus a paved area might be half the size of the lawn, and the lawn half the size of the planted areas, ratios of 1:2.

Changes of level can also divide space and create a sense of flow. But they can also play tricks with proportion. High ground has psychological as well as visual advantages. Ground that falls away seems to lengthen itself so that a garden which steps down, even a little, from one level to

the next, will seem longer than it is: but vertical features, like statues, will seem smaller than they are. Rising ground shortens distance, and makes vertical features more important than they are. A hollow draws the eye to its centre. This is exploited in sunken gardens, which often have a pond in the middle. But it can be avoided by having a grey planting in one corner, allowing the eye to drift away. A valley draws the eye along itself, leading it to whatever lies at the end of the valley.

Ground that slopes gently may be left to itself, but slopes of more than 1:2 (25°) need terracing. It is often worthwhile to create changes of level in gardens that do not slope, because of the interest they generate.

Changes in surface colour and texture create a sense of

movement. Texture is most important in those gardens in which pattern is least pronounced. Hard surfaces are most often placed by the house, where they form a visual link between house and garden, but they may extend right into the garden in the form of paths. The first function of a path is to enable one to get round the garden dry shod, but they may also lead and direct the eye. Paths should lead somewhere definite, to a seat, statue or view, or back to themselves.

Hard surfaces should be made from local materials, stone where stone is appropriate, or brick or gravel. Brick laid flat has an ugly proportion: it is better laid on edge. Bricks laid with their long axis leading away tend to seem to be disappearing: laid with their long axis across one's path they seem to slow one. Herringbone and basket-weave are non-directional. Pebbles can be pretty but are uncomfortable to walk on. Differing materials afford not only differing colours and texture, but different sounds, the silence of grass, the crunch of gravel, the crisp clip of stone flags.

More positive statements can be made by framing a surface, surrounding brick with stone, gravel with granite setts.

INTERNAL STRUCTURE

ABOVE: *Central space is emphasized by the encircling mass of plants.*

OPPOSITE: *A sculptural group consisting of the vertical Japanese lantern, evergreen mounds, and paving.*

The rhythm of a garden is primarily determined by its use of voids and solids, and the patterns these make. Voids are such open, level areas as lawns, terraces and water, but they acquire their particular quality from their juxtapositioning with solids. Solids are trees, shrubs and hedges, walls and buildings. The solids create a pattern of open and closed spaces. Primary divisions are created by solids extending above eye-level. In small gardens secondary solids, at knee-level or below, can be just as important.

Formal gardens are created by dividing the garden as though it were a series of rooms and corridors, using hedges as walls, the floor patterns being created with box-edging. In such gardens trees are planted formally in bosquets or in quincunxes, so that they create a solid clean-cut block.

In informal gardens the voids and solids flow into each other. Solid woodland gives way to a sparser planting of trees, through which the void flows; and then to a single tree punctuating the void. This enables the mind to perceive the wood both as a block of trees and as a sequence of single trees, their trunks dividing space in the same way as a colonnade, but the sequence of single trees is only effective if backed by the solidity of woodland and the openness of space.

The same principles apply in small gardens. A group will usually be improved by outriders, but single plants will only cohere if related to a group.

Dynamic Groups

Where space division is achieved by informal planting the effect can be greatly enhanced if dynamic groups are used. Such groups are an essentially sculptural use of plants, constructed from the character of the plants themselves. The principle is to marry a vertical and a horizontal by the use of a rounded shape. The archetypal combination is horizontal of a sheet of water, the vertical of a Lombardy poplar, and the rounded shape of a weeping willow. In a small garden this might translate into a small pond, the fastigiate cherry 'Amanogawa', and a shrub of *Viburnum tinus*. On a smaller scale it could be an Irish juniper, *Juniperus communis* 'Hibernica', and a cut-leafed Japanese maple on the horizontal of a lawn or terrace.

The same dynamic grouping can be achieved in the smallest of courtyard gardens, using the sword-like leaves of an iris for the vertical and the rounded mound of a hosta against the horizontal of a shelf or sill in the ground form. In the Japanese gardening tradition a similar dynamism is achieved with raked sand, a rock or a bamboo, or by using a recumbent rock for the horizontal, a bamboo for the vertical and an evergreen azalea as the unifying rounded shape.

A rhythmic arrangement of clipped yews set in a lavender hedge forms the border to a cottage path.

CLIPPED GREENS

Clipped greens can be used to divide space, emphasizing the rhythm and pattern of a garden, rather in the way colonnades are used. The best shapes for this purpose are simple geometrical ones, balls, buns, bee-skips, cones, pyramids or occasionally cubes. These divide space most effectively when they are used at regular or nearly regular intervals, equally spaced at the four imaginary corners of a circular lawn, for instance, in a row beside an unpretentious pathway or simply as a pair of markers guiding one to where the steps lead down from a terrace. Box is the best plant material

for these shapes, alluringly fragrant in summer, treasured in winter for its glossy dark greenness, indispensable for creating the winter patterns of a garden.

More complex, essentially geometric shapes can be used singly or in pairs, to create an emphasis, to underline a point. Spirals, cake-stands and poodle tails are at home among herbs or old roses. On balconies and roof gardens box may be grown in huge terracotta pots and clipped to resemble a giant green egg in its eggcup. False perspectives can be created by diminishing the stature of the specimens as they recede. More distant effects can be created with blue rue, or the mistier greys of santolina or teucrium.

Topiary birds and beasts tend to become dominant in small gardens. If one has them, one needs nothing else.

DESIGNER TREES

Pencil-thin 'designer tree', Taxus baccata 'Standishii', draws the eye in the middle of the border.

Designer trees come midway between the show specimens of the topiarist and the unruliness of a tree left to grow naturally. The problem with most trees is that they take too long to fill their design function, and then rapidly get too large. Designer trees are semi-formal freaks of nature whose shape and size seem predetermined.

Fastigiate Trees

Pencil cedars are classic designer trees. Like ex clamation marks on the horizon, they draw the eye. They can be used to lead the eye away from something unsightly in the distance, or to determine that one looks this way rather than that. Planted near intrusive telegraph poles, it is the pencil cedar you see. All fastigiate trees have this quality, from the tall Lombardy poplars through the grey *Juniperus* 'Skyrocket' to the prickly Irish juniper *J. communis* 'Hibernica'.

Round-headed Trees

Round-headed trees have the same quality of drawing the eye, perhaps because of their apparent artificiality. *Robinia pseudo-acacia* 'Inermis' is the best of these.

Its small round head is grafted onto a strong straight stem like a standard rose, so its height is predetermined. A light trim with shears in winter will keep the head to size, perhaps no more than 4ft/1.2m across. *Acer platanoides* 'Globosum' is

similar, but the head is darker in colour and more densely clad.

They can be used as markers, or to draw the eye; as specimens in tubs; in pairs to make a miniature avenue; or, planted in a formal quincunx, as a highly stylized forest.

17

A MAGNET TO THE EYE

The smaller a garden the greater the reliance on artefacts, partly because there is not space enough to provide a new flower for every season, and old foliage grows drab. In the perpetual flux of a garden artefacts may represent the stillness of eternity glimpsed elusively among mid-summer foliage or blatantly exposed in winter when frost has pushed aside the brief clothing of leaves.

Statues, seats and fountains may all be used as magnets to draw the eye, though they may also be used in other ways. Painted Old Brunswick green and placed in an arbor of greenery, a seat or statue will merge with its background: painted white it is a positive *coup d'oeil*. Fountains, by their very nature, tend to be centre-pieces in a garden, but again may be more showy, or less.

Since the eye always goes first to whatever is brightest in the field of vision, it is the luminosity of a statue or seat or other artefact that first draws the eye to it. What then holds the eye is some sense of recognition and familiarity, the human shape of a statue, the rhythm and repetition of man-made objects, the sheer enigma of abstract forms. Such strong visual impact needs to be carefully controlled. It needs to be placed deliberately at the end of a vista or at the centre of a garden or border where it may act as a fulcrum. Lead statuary, less luminous, can play a quieter role and may be concealed round a corner to be often forgotten and frequently refound, a lesser incident.

Seats, to be restful, must belong. They should look as though they have been there

Pair of white seats set beneath a delicate white arbour act as a magnet to the eye.

Apples in the lap of the seated girl make her part of the autumnal garden.

so long they have taken root. Stone seats have the advantage of sheer weight, but even the flimsiest of seats will look as though it belongs if it is placed on a plinth of brick or stone, and embraced by an alcove of hedging or placed under an arbor.

Statues should belong too, but in a different sense: they should express the spirit of the place. Because they compel the eye, they must be exactly right.

Statues have had a place in gardens since classical times, when their original significance was sacred. In these more profane times their prime function is to draw the eye, though like any work of art they should also delight. Other objects will draw the eye as well: stone gateposts, mill stones, sundials, wine and cider presses, ornate chimney pots or the fluted columns from some once baronial hall. Nymphs and satyrs, left over from the glory that was Greece, look sadly out of place in colder, greyer climes, encrusted with lichens and caught naked in the cold winter rain.

But statuary and sculpture are about more than merely literary ideas: they are contrasts of form and texture, mass and void. The illusion of movement is created by the play of light and shade: in abstract forms space seems to flow. Scale is crucial. A statue that seems huge indoors, set out in the garden may seem insignificant. Too large a sculpture will dominate; too small a sculpture will be lost among the foliage. Too many sculptures confuse the eye and the mind: unless several form a single group, or one is obviously more important than the others.

Wooden pergola with the roses 'Wedding Day', 'Bleu Magenta' and 'Botany Bay' underplanted with nepeta.

ARMATURES

Armatures are those garden structures over which may be grown plants that without support would simply sprawl on the ground. Such structures are indispensable for creating a sense of vertical space in small gardens where trees might grow too large or too fast. Their advantage over trees is that they are of fixed dimensions, and such annual growths as exceed the framework may easily be removed.

Colonnades and Arches

The archetypal garden armature is the colonnade, a sequence of poles or pillars spaced at equal intervals along an axis, and linked together at the top by poles or swags of rope or iron. A pergola is a pair of parallel colonnades linked across the top with further poles. The spacing of the uprights of a pergola offers the opportunity to look out from shade into sunlight, always a pleasing experience. A tunnel, by contrast, is closed at the sides (and usually rounded overhead) so that one's eye is guided from the entrance through the tunnel to whatever lies beyond. These devices are

A tall narrow wooden quadripod supports the climbing rose 'Mme. Driout'.

bright suns. In medieval Europe pergolas were essentially rustic in character, made of hazel boughs lashed together, but by the high Renaissance they had become carpenter's work, with barrel-vaulted arches overhead. Only in the twentieth century under the influence of the architect Sir Edwin Lutyens, have pergolas become architectural rather than horticultural features, with massive pillars and huge beams overhead.

It is necessary to decide whether the climber or the structure is the more important. If the structure itself is designed to enchant it can be light and delicate. If it is the plants that matter a more substantial structure is needed. A mature wisteria can be as heavy as a full grown tree. Colonnades are most often made simply of short upright poles linked with swags of rope or chains, but pergolas need to be stronger. Brick pillars and transverse members are strong and effective, but a different idiom can be created by using stone pillars and curving the timbers overhead so that each pair of pillars becomes an arch. A different effect is achieved if you use cast-iron pillars with an iron framework overhead, though it is doubtful whether plants are so happy growing over metal structures.

The colour of these armatures is also important. Painted white they draw the eye. Most plants will look best if the armature is painted to play a supporting role, dark grey or black, or verdigris.

strongly directional. An arbour, by contrast, is static, a place of repose.

Arches, which may be as simple as a honeysuckle over a bent hazel stick, have a special potency, being an ever-open doorway between one garden experience and another.

A single upright pole may support a clematis and rose. Three poles lashed together make a tripod. Or four may form a quadripod or pyramid,

though pyramids are usually more formal and clad in trellis.

Pergolas

Such structures originated in classical times simply as another means of supporting the grape-vine, but they soon evolved into a method of creating those shaded walks so beloved of those who live in hot climates under the glare of

Wisteria

One of the joys of a small garden is that one has time to cherish one's plants in a way that would be quite impossible in a larger garden. Most of the finest plants for growing on armatures need such care.

Wisteria are generally considered the most desirable of all climbers, with delicate leaflets and long pendent racemes of usually fragrant, usually mauve, pea-shaped flowers. Most, if properly pruned, flower in three to four years from planting. Initially train the long thin shoots to form a framework over the armature. Once that is achieved prune all long growths back to their first two leaves, after flowering and again in winter: or prune all summer. Even the most vigorous species can be kept quite small in this way.

W. *sinensis* is generally most reliable, producing its 12in/30cm long racemes of fragrant mauve or white flowers in late spring, and briefly again in late summer. W. *floribunda* flowers at the same season and has, in addition to mauve, a form with pink flowers, 'Rosea' (lovely with the deeper pink clematis 'Hagley Hybrid'), a double, deep violet form, 'Violacea Plena' and a form 'Multijuga', legendary for the length of its racemes, often 3ft/1m or more. W. *japonica* is useful for extending the season, producing its yellowish-white to white flowers in later summer.

Clematis

Known in a more decorous age as Virgin's bower, these will, if you feed them weekly and give them a gallon of water a day in summer, produce a succession of flowers from late winter to the end of autumn, needing very little ground space. In a quarter of an acre one can grow, with proper pruning, ten wisterias and about fifty clematis.

A few, like the late winter-flowering pale green and red-spotted C. *balearica* 'Freckles', and the spring-flowering C. *montana* in its pink and white forms and the opulent but untidy evergreen C. *armandii* are so vigorous they will cover a pergola on their own, but

ABOVE: Clematis viticella 'Purpurea Plena' flowers abundantly from late summer onwards.
OPPOSITE: Wisteria can be grown as a standard or over a frame.

most are best grown up through other plants, either to flower together or to overlap. The popular C. 'Nelly Moser' and the similar C. 'Bees Jubilee' with their pink flowers with darker bands are lovely with the mauve wisterias which flower in late spring. C. 'Hagley Hybrid' echoes the colour of the pink wisteria, W. *floribunda* 'Rosea', in a deeper tone. The sumptuous C. 'W.E. Gladstone' with lavender sepals and red anthers has sufficient depth of colour to tone with the darkest of wisterias, W. *sinensis* 'Black Dragon'. C. *viticella* and its forms flower from summer till autumn, in hues that blend with old roses and lavenders. C. *viticella* 'Polish Spirit' is a yellow-stamened deep purple, lovely over-lapping and following on from the pink Bourbon rose 'Blairii No.2'. C.v. 'Purpurea Plena' is sumptuously dark, like black opals, and makes a lovely show with the dense, misty-mauve heads of *Allium pyrenaicum*, *Platycodon* 'Mother of Pearl' and the lavender 'Seale' backed by *Berberis* × *ottawensis* 'Silver Miles'. C.v. 'Kermesina' is crimson and 'Abundance' soft purple.

Those clematis which flower after mid-summer should be cut nearly to the ground in late winter. All others should only be trimmed lightly to tidy them.

Isaac Periere', the most popular of the Bourbons, producing its rich pink, highly scented flowers from midsummer till the frosts, with the double-flowered clematis 'Vyvyan Pennell' and the silver-grey lavenders 'Hidcote' or 'Twickel Purple'. Roses are most floriferous when the flow of sap is restricted. Bind rose stems up poles or round the beams of a pergola and they will produce even more flower.

Other Options

A completely different effect, like a pool of sunlight on even the dullest days, can be produced by the golden hop, *Humulus lupulus* 'Aureus' on an armature, its sharper lemony tones echoed by the huge heads of *Euphorbia wulfenii* 'Lambrook Gold', with a greeny-yellow froth of Lady's Mantle, *Alchemilla mollis*, at its feet, and lime-green nicotianas to follow through till the frosts.

In theory any tree, shrub or climber whose flowers or fruits are pendulous could be trained over a framework to form an arch or tunnel, the leafage being on the outside, the fruits or flowers hanging down inside the roof of the tunnel. In practice, the laburnum is so showy when

Roses

Climbers are generally best for growing over structures, as ramblers, with the exception of Multifloras, are mostly too vigorous. Choose colours that blend with nearby walls or brickwork, and then build colour co-ordinated groupings. The rose 'Gloire de Dijon' which produces its fragrant, quartered buff-yellow suffused with pink and apricot flowers all summer in sun or shade, often goes well with brick-

work. It makes a lovely group with the foxglove 'Suttons Apricot', the peachy-apricot *Iris* 'Prairie Sunrise' and the tulip 'Apricot Beauty'. The deep pink rose 'Zéphirine Drouhin' is better with bricks of a bluer tint, and looks well with the rich blue clematis 'Lady Northcliffe', purple foxgloves, *Geraniums* 'Buxton's Blue' and white 'Sylvaticum Album' and the hostas 'Halcyon' and 'Hadspen Blue' both with glaucous-blue leaves. Or, further from the house, the rose 'Mme.

used like this that few people desire anything else. Its flexible branches are easily tied into position and it needs little routine thinning. The finest laburnum for this purpose is *L. × watereri* 'Vossii' with streamers of flowers 2ft/60cm long. The golden laburnum, *L. anagyroides* 'Aureum' has yellow leaves all summer. Robinias can be trained in the same way and have grape-like bunches of scented pink or white flowers. In cottage gardens, the common hazel,

often grown for its nuts, can be trained to make a tunnel which in spring is clothed inside with catkins.

Climbers can be used to create height at the back of a bed or border. A single stout, stripped pole, 4in/10cm thick, sunk 2ft/60cm into the ground with 7ft/2.1m or more above ground and clad in a sheath of coarse-mesh chicken wire will provide an ideal support for a rose, clematis or honeysuckle. The English shrub rose 'Leander' with deep apricot flowers and the

yellow honeysuckle 'Graham Stuart Thomas' blend, and are of matching vigour. Rose 'Rêve d'Or' is more coppery, and rose 'Schoolgirl' pinker. Both go well with the yellow-variegated summer jasmine, *Jasminum officinale* 'Aureo-variegatum'.

A single pole may also support, for winter effect, an ivy, preferably variegated. Large-leafed variegated ivies such as *Hedera colchica* 'Variegata' or *H. canariensis* 'Gloire de Marengo' also contribute a distinctive foliage.

25

A dark pot and plinth for a deep bronze cordyline.

POTS, TUBS AND CASES

Choosing pots, tubs and cases requires as much care as the choice of plants or the design of one's garden. Generally these *jardinières* play a supporting role to the plants, though there are times and places where their role as sculptural forms is more important, in which case they remain unplanted.

The simplest pots are best for displays of flowering plants. Highly decorated pots embellished with swags of fruit or flowers are better used with foliage plants. Avoid ornate planting in ornate pots, unless that is the effect you seek. Old-fashioned everyday terracotta shows off flowers to perfec-

tion. There is nothing better. The colour and brightness of highly glazed pots tend to compete with the flowers. Narrow-necked pots are likely to look absurd with a tuft of greenery sprouting out of the top.

Tubs should be simple in shade and colour, the bleached grey of natural wood, or white with black ironwork. Strong colours limit the choice of flowers, but may themselves sometimes extend a colour theme from the house. *Caisses de Versailles*

Colour-coordinated plants cascade from simple terracotta pots beside the seat; Geranium
palmatum *is on the left, pelargoniums on the right.*

(Versailles tubs) are best
planted with a single solid
object, clipped bays, yews or
myrtles, or more dramati-
cally, *Brugmansia* (syn.
Datura) *suaveolens.*

Use soil-based potting
mixes, and feed plants daily
throughout the summer.

Siting Pots and Tubs

Pots and tubs are often
most telling when used
on the area that links the
house with the garden,

because they carry the fam-
iliar scale of household things
out into the garden. This
sense of unity can be
reinforced by using similar
pots inside and out, or similar
plants. *Fatsia japonica* for
example, can be grown in-
doors or out, as can lilies,
bamboos, and aspidistras.

Consideration must be
given to where the pots and
their plants will be seen from
most often. If it is from the
house, it is important to
ensure that the planting of
the pots does not compete

with the garden beyond. As
the foreground of the picture
viewed from the house, the
pots and their plants will be
dominant. In a small town
garden they may provide all
the flowers that are needed,
and it may be best to set out
the rest of the garden in a
quiet idiom of green grass
and evergreens, box edging
or prostrate junipers at
the sides, lapping against the
wall like waves. Never be
afraid of simplicity. Reti-
cence is the hallmark of
elegance.

27

Box balls in blue and white painted pots in a densely planted corner of a tiny city garden.

One thing all good gardens have in common is a sense of imposing order on chaos. For this reason pots are most effective when they have some common factor, size, shape or colour, or are deliberately chosen as variations on a theme. More often one collects an odd assortment of pots over the years, and these can be given unity by their arrangement on the ground, and by the planting scheme. For example, one might plant the largest pot with the pelargonium 'Apple Blossom' whose double pink flowers have just a hint of blue, and surround this with smaller pots planted with one shade of pink Busy Lizzie, and white ones, the two pinks matching but in different tones: or use semperflorens begonias, which will flourish in the shade.

Planting Schemes

Schemes may be simple or complex. One plant per pot may be too simple to satisfy unless one plants six or eight pots with the same plant and then groups them together. Gertrude Jekyll used to plant pots full of the August lily (*Hosta plantaginea*) whose long-tubed white flowers are one of the most fragrant joys of summer, and group them behind pots full of *Francoa ramosa* whose upright wands of spidery white flowers and hairy leaves were in complete contrast to the hosta. *H. plantaginea* is a sun lover but most hostas are shade lovers and are ideal for pots in shade, grouped with pots of ferns and large tubs of hydrangeas. Ferns like *Polystichum setiferum divisilobum* and the various forms of *Dryopteris*

Winter furnishing: the simplicity of a potted evergreen myrtle set among conifers.

Argyranthemum 'Rollason's Red', using fuchsias such as the scarlet and violet 'Mrs Popple' and the soft pink, ivy-leafed pelargonium 'Mme. Crousse' and 'Lady Plymouth' with scented cream and green leaves. These can be combined with the eponymous Verbena 'Imperial Purple' and 'Silver Anne' in shades of light and medium pinks, together with Plecostachys serpyllifolia. Such a scheme associates well with old roses.

Tubs and half-barrels can be treated in the same way, but also lend themselves to a quite different treatment. They hold enough soil to grow a whole succession of flowers. The essence is to plant bulbs round a central woody specimen, those bulbs that flower earliest nearest the top of the soil. The succession is snowdrops, crocus, early dwarf narcissus then taller, larger flowered daffodils, and finally tulips, taking the season into May.

The central specimen must give winter colour, a variegated holly or standard euonymus, and some variation in the colour scheme is possible. 'Golden King' holly or Euonymus 'Emerald 'n' Gold' would go well with golden crocuses, golden daffodils and tulips such as 'Golden Harvest'. Alternatively 'Silver Queen' holly or Euonymus 'Emerald Gaiety' goes with an all-white sequence, using daffodils such as 'Thalia'. The planting should be done in the early autumn, and the soil renewed each year.

filix-mas are ideal. Hosta fortunei and its forms, the white-margined 'Francee' and the yellow-edged H.f. 'Aureo-marginata' are excellent, as is the glaucous H. 'Halcyon'. Hydrangeas can readily be blued in tubs or kept pink by the addition of lime. The polystichum remains green in winter and a good companion would be the Christmas box, Sarcococca confusa, with small shiny evergreen leaves and fragrant white flowers, like pips of lilacs, in mid-winter.

Where only a single large pot or tub, or a matching pair are to be used, each can be a work of art in itself. The first essential is to settle on a colour theme, and then select the plants to fill it. A yellow, white and grey scheme, for example, might be planted using a semi-standard of the white-flowered, grey-leafed marguerite or Paris daisy, Argyranthemum frutescens, Bidens ferulifolia which provides brilliant yellow daisy flowers, and soft yellow Helichrysum petiolare 'Limelight', as well as the grey, tiny-leafed Plecostachys serpyllifolia.

A successful pink and mauve scheme can be made around the Paris daisy

ABOVE: *Balcony garden with container plants.*

RIGHT: *Dark green and white roof garden with clipped evergreens in an elongated box; it will look cool in summer, clothed in winter.*

BALCONIES AND ROOF GARDENS

*B*alconies call for even more care in the choice of containers for every detail tells. Square or rectangular containers, that fit together well, optimize available space. Pots and planting should give the illusion that the room extends into a bower beyond. A pair of pots inside might be echoed outside to foster the illusion. Use trellis screwed to the house wall as supports for roses, clematis, summer jasmine or ivies, grown in large pots. These will peep round the corners of the windows alluringly.

The most colour can be obtained by alternating blocks of successional plantings which, as mentioned on the previous page, give colour from spring till summer, with areas of all-summer flowering plantings as mentioned on the previous two pages. An extra sense of depth and unity can be obtained if the planting schemes extend the colours of the room, or pick up colours from the curtains. Height adds a further dimension, and can be quickly achieved with bamboos (which can also be grown inside).

Roof gardens offer more scope, but are also more limited. If you have any fears about the weight of soil a roof can carry, check with an architect or structural engineer. Wind is also a limiting factor, and its force should

not be underestimated.

One of the prime design functions of a garden is to link the house to the land it stands on. On a roof garden, where plants are so far removed from the earth to which they belong, the garden must be a self-referring system, entire in itself.

The essence of a roof garden is that one should feel in it not on it. Hedges can be planted in long narrow containers, like overgrown window-boxes, to form the perimeter. Hedges are gross

feeders and need regular supplies of fertilizer. Arbours and arches to frame a view or make a sitting area can be made of strong trellis on stout supports fixed to roof joists. These, together with the hedges, can provide sufficient height to bring a sense of security. Planting should be essentially simple and renewable. A few permanent shrubs give continuity. Trees are inappropriate so far above the ground, but a few designer trees might be used to represent them, grown in tubs or *caisses de Versailles*.

The limitations of a roof garden – the fact that everything has to be grown in flower boxes – tends to lead towards formality in design but the straight lines can be broken up by the use of occasional large pots. A miscellany of pot-grown greenery, on the other hand, may never cohere into a garden.

Water can be used to dramatic effect on a roof, bringing the intense play of light into the garden. Illusions are in order. A raised tank may appear to be

12in/30cm or 16in/40cm deep, but may only contain 2in/5cm of water. That is sufficient to bring a reflection of the sky down into the garden, or for a fountain to play upon. Pools that are to contain fish or plants must have a smaller surface area to compensate for the extra depth and weight. An enchanting little water feature can be made in a well caulked half-barrel. It is large enough for a fish, a fountain and a small water lily, together with some oxygenating weed.

31

ABOVE: Formal pool given extra definition by the surround of blue-painted tubs at its corners.
OPPOSITE: Even the tiniest yard could find room for these miniature water gardens in stone troughs.

WATER

Water is the soul of a garden. Without it a garden lacks life and movement. Such vitality does it bestow that it should always be considered a major feature in the design, even when it occupies a relatively small area.

In gardens which seek to create a natural effect the water should lie easily in the contours, at the lowest point, as though it had settled there. Such waters will appear larger if the banks slope gently down because they will reflect a larger area of sky: steep banks cast shadows which reduce the reflective area. In a wide open space water will reflect the whole arch of the sky and appear bright: but if it is enclosed by crowding evergreens it will seem mysteriously deepened and darkened, and will reflect only the deep blue of the zenith overhead. Such naturalistic waters are best left still, reflecting surrounding trees and flowers.

In formal gardens the water should be contained in tanks or pools of essentially geometric shape, and the water should always be as high in its container as possible. The pool may be nearer the house than with naturalistic pools, but should have plenty of ground visible beyond it, to avoid the illusion of the pool slipping away over the edge of the garden. Alternatively strong verticals will anchor it.

Such a pool may be designed to reflect an arch or statue lying beyond it, but at night it might be enlivened by submerged lights and agitated by the play of fountains. Very formal pools edged with stone or slabs and with fountains are best set in plain, mown grass. Flowers would distract the eye. Simplicity is endlessly fascinating.

The planting of pools needs to be restrained. If the whole surface is covered with vegetation the point of the pool is lost. As a general rule not more than a third of the surface area should be covered. The best effects are achieved with fewest plants. The round pads of water lilies emphasize the horizontal nature of water: sword-like leaves of water irises or typhas provide a counterbalancing vertical: while a froth of parrot's feather, Myriophyllum aquaticum, with its lace-like, grey-green leaves, softens the whole effect. There are miniature water lilies for tiny pools, and dwarf typhas.

ASPECT

When a garden designer walks into a garden he has never seen before he automatically orients himself by the sun and starts thinking in terms of, for example, roses and lavender in the sun, ferns, hostas and hellebores in the shade, of plants for a wall that receives morning or, conversely, afternoon sun, and how to harmonize all these elements. These are crucial observations that have to be made on every site. However, in small gardens, and especially very small town gardens, the overall sunniness or shadiness may be even more important. Small, sunny walled gardens absorb heat from the sun by day and give it off again by night, and so one can grow tender plants other gardeners only dream of: but the same garden, sunless, may be cold and dank and need special care in planting.

Soil is equally important, for many plants specifically need well-drained soils, while others will tolerate clays. Similarly, some plants, rhododendrons and camellias for example, need acid soil, while gypsophila and pinks are best on chalky soils.

No aspect is intrinsically good or bad. Successful gardens may be made in any aspect provided that one suits the plants to the place and works in an appropriate palette, for the flowers which flourish in the shade come in quieter hues than those which thrive in the sun.

Hot sunny terrace emphasizes the contrast between light and shade.

The house always dictates the style of its garden, as in Sissinghurst's cottage garden.

SIMPLICITY OF PURPOSE

Once the aspect of the garden is known, its general layout and planting can be considered. A pool is best in sun, but a terrace for sitting on may be in sun or shade. Decisions about these things need to be made as much in relation to one's lifestyle and how the garden is to be used as in regard to the orientation, but the orientation will largely determine the plants you can employ.

The house sets the style. Traditional old roses and lavender are best with traditional houses, while modern houses marry best with modern gardens of grasses and yuccas, the golden-rayed flowers of *Rudbeckia fulgida* and *Sedum spectabile* with its flat pink heads. Each would look wrong with the other. A cottage garden, with its exuberant infor-

mality, would look as much out of place around a Georgian mansion with its simple classic formality as would a garden of pure Cartesian formality seem ill-suited to a mud-and-wattle thatched cottage. Appropriateness of style is the key-note.

The next decisions concern the basic colour theme or themes of the garden. The starting point is always the house and its colours. Paintwork can, if need arises, be changed to suit a colour scheme, but brickwork remains as it is, so that the colours must harmonize with that. Generally the most enjoyable small gardens are those made around a single colour theme, or a single theme to each compartment. Miss Jekyll used to speak of "simplicity of purpose", by which she meant that if you are going to make a yellow or blue garden, make it yellow and blue and subordinate everything to achieving that single effect: don't dissipate it by admitting a stray pink or orange. Concentrate your effects.

RHYTHM, PATTERN AND REPETITION

If one were to persuade a concert pianist and a builder's labourer to play a single note on a piano the differences would be scarcely distinguishable. But get them to play a run of eight or ten notes and the difference would be immediately apparent, for the musician would so arrange his notes that they were pleasing to the ear, whether a scale, a broken chord or a fragment of a tune, whereas the labourer would strike notes at random creating more dissonance than delight. It is the same with gardening. The beginner puts in his plants at random, a few associating happily, but most making uncomfortable com-panions, whereas the experi-enced gardener will see at once what goes with what and which does not.

The musical analogies do not end there. Gardens, like music, have melodies as well as rhythm, andantes as well as allegros, vivace and lente, and crescendos as well as diminuendos. They move from one theme to another and then return to the original theme, but vary the theme rather than merely repeating it. Indeed, when

ABOVE: *Silver plants are the space-makers between groups of bronze fennels.*

LEFT: *Repeated planting seen in a trio of silver verbascums at the front of a border.*

making a garden it is useful to think of it in sonata form, with the themes stated and then elaborated and interwoven with other themes.

Rhythm

The first thing is to establish the rhythm of the garden, its basic beat. Anything that is repeated at regular intervals will do this, whether plants or the poles of a pergola. When the eye looks down a bed or border it is drawn first to the line that divides the bed or border from the lawn or paving in which it is set. For this reason plants are most tellingly used to create the rhythm of a border when they are placed right at the front. And since the eye goes next to the most luminous plants (those lightest in colour) plants with grey foliage are ideal space makers, *Stachys byzantina*, for example, or *Brachyglottis* (syn. *Senecio*) 'Sunshine', dianthus or garden pinks, some artemisias, and *Hebe pagei*. But the eye is also drawn to uprights, and the garden designer Lanning Roper used to use the grey, upright, sword-like leaves of tall bearded irises at the front of borders to create their basic rhythm. Lavenders also combine greyness with upright spikes of flowers, but in a less obvious idiom, as does nepeta, and many of the salvias, *S. superbum*, for example.

These markers will further affect the rhythm depending upon whether the plants are used as staccato singles or in groups, of threes or fives or sevens, or interwoven with other plants.

The shape of the markers varies in effect. Upright shapes, such as Irish yews, are more emphatic than low rounded mushroom-shaped mounds. Again, they are more emphatic when grown in the grass beside a bed or border than when grown in the border itself, merging at least in part with the other vegetation.

One might, for example, decide to repeat plantings of mauve *Nepeta mussinii* at the front of a border of old roses, using it rather like bars in music, to create a sense of space and rhythm. A more interesting way of looking at it is as one of three themes that always occur together, in clusters, the other two being the pink rose 'The Fairy' and Stachys byzantina. If we denote the nepeta as A, the rose as B and the stachys as C, then the grouping can be varied at each repetition, as ABC, ACB, BAC, CBA and so on. On a different colour theme the combination of Lady's Mantle (Alchemilla mollis) with its lax heads of tiny lime-green flowers, Geranium × magnificum with its vibrant mauve-blue flowers and Achillea grandifolia with its grey leaves and flat heads of nearly white flowers, might be used.

ABOVE: Pastel repetitions with cream eschscholzia and sisyrinchium.

RIGHT: A link is made between the mauve Clematis 'Vyvyan Pennell' and the purple sage, drawing background and foreground together. The rose 'Easlea's Golden Rambler' is the luminous intervention.

These clusters of plants are sufficient in themselves to give a border cohesion, the desired sense of rhythm, pattern and repetition. But one could go on to develop an entire bed, border or garden as interlocking variations on a theme. One might for example, at the back of the border where one has at the front the nepeta, the rose 'The Fairy' and Stachys byzantina, employ the cluster Berberis × ottawensis 'Silver Miles', the Reverend Pemberton's hybrid musk rose 'Felicia' (a pale pink) and the old English lavender 'Seale', mainly for its silveryness, for its flowers are of ghostly paleness.

If these are then denoted as D, E and F they can be varied within the cluster in the same way as the ABC theme. A further minor linking theme in this border might be composed of Platycodon grandiflora 'Mother of Pearl', the soft mauve Allium pyrenaicum and Campanula 'Hidcote Amethyst', a grouping which would be too insubstantial on its own and which depends for its effectiveness on the stronger colours around it.

Similarly the yellow, blue and white theme (respectively, Alchemilla mollis, Geranium × magnificum and Achillea grandifolia) could have behind it an interlocking theme of Phlomis samia (syn. P. russelliana) with grey rounded leaves and whorls of yellow flowers, delphiniums in mauvish tones and the tall thin white spires of Verbascum chaixii, again varied within the cluster, with a foreground sub-theme of Convolvulus sabatius with its clear blue saucer-flowers and Sisyrinchium striatum 'Aunt May', with its spires of primrose blooms and cream-and-green striped leaves.

In looser schemes, in wild gardens, the rhythm markers need not always be the same plant. It is enough to repeat grey foliage. This might be Brachyglottis (syn. Senecio) 'Sunshine', or Salix hastata or S. lanata, one of the grey-leafed forms of Rhododendron viscosum, or even hostas or Petasites paradoxus. At its simplest the rhythm of a garden may be asserted by the alternation of voids and solids, even though the particular solids differ. Shrubs might act as markers in a border of perennials.

Pattern

Pattern is implicit in all garden design. It is there in the layout of paths and hedges, in the disposition of beds and borders and in the final shape of the lawn. The extent to which the patterns become explicit or remain implicit largely determines the style of the garden. The more explicit the pattern the more formal the garden, the less explicit the more informal. The knots and parterres of the Italian villas and the formal French gardens are pure pattern: in the English landscape garden pattern is no more than merely implied and often not perceived – the alternation of void and solid, of woodland and grassland.

The simplest patterns consist of a motif repeated along an axis, as for example when grey foliage is repeated along the front of a border. Bi-lateral symmetry, as in an avenue, reinforces the sense of pattern.

The patterns found in *parterres de broderie* are different in kind, as are the knots still used in herb gardens, being of a different order of complexity. The old gardening books are full of patterns for such knots and parterres, yet when re-created they have little more than historic interest. More dynamic knots can be created where one invents one's own patterns. The contemporary idiom is simpler. The compartments are no longer filled with red brick dust and black granite chippings but rather with coloured-leafed plants such as *Heuchera* 'Palace Purple' or *Berberis thun-bergii* 'Atropurpurea Nana' or santolina clipped flat at the same height as the box hedge (known as table-tops). Teucrium and lavender can be used in the same way. In minimalist gardens, by contrast, pattern is created by the use of only a single species of tree, each echoing all the others, a re-interpretation perhaps of the *bosquets* of André Le Nôtre.

The Use of Colour

All colour comes about because a surface such as a flower reflects some of the light that falls on it, and absorbs the rest. A red flower reflects red light, and absorbs all other light: a blue flower reflects blue light and absorbs the rest. Black absorbs all light: white reflects it all. The

A brilliant colour association of a burnt-red mimulus and a blue campanula; each reflects its own colour light and absorbs all others.

Contrasting forms of flowers: the double trinity of the Iris 'Brasilia' and the starry spire of camassia.

nearer to white a colour is the more luminous it will appear: the nearer to black the darker. If you sit in a garden in the evening as the light fades around you, you will find that the first colours to disappear are deep blues and mauves and violets, then the darker reds and greens. Pinks and pale creamy colours linger longer, but white outlasts them all. In the border, whites and pale colours advance to meet you: dark colours recede. You can so manipulate your colour chords as to make the border look longer.

In the scheme *Stachys byzantina* = A, the rose 'The Fairy' = B and *Nepeta mussinii* = C, rather than varying the theme ABC, ACB, BCA, CBA and so on, which is really just a matter of rotation, one can vary the composition of the chord so that it has more light colours nearer the house, more dark colours further away: for example, ABA, ABC, BAB, CBC. This grades the chord from lighter (and nearer) to darker (and further). The same can be done with the sub-themes, to enhance the effect.

A further refinement is to vary the size and form of the flowers. Peonies and oriental poppies produce huge flowers, great blobs of colour. Gypsophila and *Crambe cordifolia* produce tiny flowers, but in vast quantity. Each contributes to the overall effect in the garden in

different ways, the finer flowers acting as a foil for the larger. Not only do the actual flowers offer an amazing diversity of forms, the trumpets of the lilies, the disc and ray arrangement of the daisies, the cup and saucer of the campanulas, the double-trinity form of the irises and so on, but also in the clusters in which they are presented: the squat pyramids of lupins, the flat heads of the achilleas, the round heads of alliums or agapanthus, the cylindrical heads of euphorbias. It is not necessary to thematize these in the border, but rather consciously to make the effort to vary them, for we all tend to fall into favouring one form of flower or another, trumpet or daisy, pea or umbellifer.

GARDENING IN LAYERS

Most of us when we come to lay out a garden tend to think of it as flat, an area of ground surface to be beautified. In fact the vertical space above the ground is just as much a part of the garden, and it is essential to use it too, not only to create a long display of colour but also to bring into play this extra dimension. The model is climatic climax temperate forest. The tall trees shelter the understorey of shrubs: the shrubs shelter herbaceous plants: and the ground itself is full of bulbs. There may also be climbers, using the ligneous strength of the trees to support their scandent limbs, and epiphytes, such as ferns and orchids, festooning the crotches and branches of the trees.

In a small garden one tree is often enough, in which case it needs to be a tree for all seasons. The false camellia tree, *Stuartia pseudocamellia*, comes close to the ideal. In spring the unfurling leaves are copper-coloured, becoming bright, light green all summer. It produces its white fragrant flowers in high summer, when few other trees are in flower: it has brilliant autumn colours – flames and scarlets. And then in winter its multi-coloured stem becomes the main attraction. It needs acid soil to flourish.

Other multi-season trees include the *Malus*, most of which flower in spring and flush with colour in the autumn and carry a crop of fruits into the winter. Many of the *Sorbus* are similarly of interest in flower, in leaf, autumn colour and fruit. Both are suitable for small gardens, and will grow in a wide variety of soils.

Some trees contribute a single feature of such beauty that one could almost shape a garden round them. The mahogany cherry, *Prunus serrula*, has bark that peels in horizontal bands to reveal a stem that looks like old and deeply polished mahogany. Its leaves are greyish, and its small white flowers fleeting and insignificant. Sometimes it is possible to buy 'Chippendale Cherries', which have the same lovely bark, but a cherry with showier flowers grafted on top. *Prunus maackii*, the Manchurian cherry, has similar bark but is a taller tree.

Sometimes, the foliage of a tree may be sufficient. The golden catalpa, *C. bignonioides* 'Aurea', has large heart-shaped leaves of a rich golden colour, creating a pool of warm sunlight. Once established, its stems can be clothed with a small-leafed golden ivy to create winter interest.

Or the shape of the tree may be paramount, the plot demanding a fastigiate tree (like the deciduous *Prunus* 'Amanogawa' or the slim hawthorn, *Crataegus monogyna* 'Stricta', or the conifers *Juniperus virginiana* 'Skyrocket', or *Thuja occidentalis* 'Malonyana'); or a horizontal (*Cornus controversa*, *Viburnum tomentosum*, *Juniperus sabina* 'Tamariscifolia') or weeping. The classic weeping tree for small

ABOVE: The tree forms the topmost layer over shrubs, roses and herbaceous plants like valerian and the blue Campanula poscharskyana adhering to the base of its trunk.

RIGHT: The varnished mahogany trunk of Prunus serrula is its distinguishing feature.

The grey-leafed weeping pear, Pyrus salicifolia 'Pendula', (to the right) droops down from the other side of the wall.

gardens is the weeping silver pear *Pyrus salicifolia* 'Pendula', which however only reveals its habit if trained up with a leader and if its lower branches are re-moved to a height of 7ft/2.1m. Otherwise it looks like an overgrown crow's nest on the ground.

The shrub layer frames the main picture. In formal layouts the shrubs may be clipped, as with yew hedges and box edging, but they still serve the same design function. The herbaceous plants, the perennials, may provide most of the colour in the garden, but they should still be subservient to the shrubs. The bulb layer can pop up under bare shrubs, or in the place occupied by a peony.

Successive Layers

Very often it is possible to create schemes in which the layers occur not only in space, but also in time, each layer larger than the one before, the smallest first. One might, for example, start in spring with a carpet of sky-blue grape hyacinth (*Muscari armeniacum*) or scillas (*Scilla sibirica*). While these are still in flower the next period of interest is already emerging, the red stems of peonies and the yellow stems of Crown Imperials (*Fritillaria imperialis*). The crown imperials flower first, but then fade rapidly away so that it is the big bold flowers of the peonies that hold sway in early mid-summer. The next layer might be either phlox which flower mid-summer or Japanese anemones (*Anemone* × *hybrida*) which flower late summer. The final autumn layer may have to be smaller rather than larger and grown at the front of the border – drifts of Kaffir lilies (*Schizostylis coccinea* and its forms) with their grassy leaves and spikes of red, pink or white flowers or, where the climate is too inclement for these, colchicums which produce their chalices of mauve flowers from the bare ground, the large leaves following in spring.

In a minute courtyard garden the layers might be, at their simplest, a small semi-weeping tree such as *Gleditsia triacanthos* 'Bujotii' with frond-like foliage or a wisteria trained over an iron umbrella;

Sarcococca confusa, a dense glossy-leaved evergreen bush which produces fragrant white flowers in winter; a sprawling osteosperum or the soft coral *Diascia rigescens* to give flower all summer paired with the stiff ever-green sword-like leaves of *Iris foetidissima* to give a vertical accent, set in a carpet of *Lamium maculatum* 'Beacon Silver', through which snowdrops and clumps of early daffodils appear in spring.

Given more space, the bulk of the small tree needs to be anchored to the ground by a counterbalancing large bush, preferably evergreen, *Mahonia japonica*, perhaps, or *Fatsia japonica*, *Viburnum tinus* or one of the plain-leafed aucubas. If more than

one tree is to be used, then thought needs to be given to the ways in which those trees will modify the habitats of the plants around them. The ground in front of a tree (on its sunny side) will be hot and dry, ideal for bulbs which like a summer baking, and for Mediterranean plants, spurges, cistus, halimium, while the far side will be in shade for part of the day (since the shade follows the sun), but this amounts to no more than half shade. If two trees are planted 7 – 10ft/ 2.1 – 3m apart, then there will be a triangle of shade between them, the hypotenuse of the triangle being a line between their stems. In such an area ferns, hostas and hellebores might thrive.

Shady garden with ferns and small seat partly sheltered by the tree's canopy of foliage.

SOME BASIC GROUPINGS

It is perfectly possible to garden in layers in co-ordinated colours. It helps to have a firm grasp of the main sorts of plants that perform at each season. The gardener's season begins at the end of autumn, that last stage before winter, when all the leaves have fallen from the trees, and the berries are fast disappearing.

The Winter Group

The first flowers of the new season are usually provided by the autumn cherry, *Prunus subhirtella* 'Autumnalis', which flowers in late autumn and intermittently

through winter. With it flowers the scented yellow *Mahonia* 'Charity' (the shrub layer). *Iris foetidissima* (the perennial layer) contributes the orange of its seeds, while the bulb layer is filled by *Cyclamen coum*, pink, white or crimson. The winter scene can be filled out where space permits with coppiced, colour-stemmed dogwoods and willows, under-planted with *Euonymus* 'Emerald 'n' Gold' and 'Silver Queen', silver and gold variegated ivies, with box or Chinese box (*Sarcococca*) or *Viburnum davidii* to provide rich contrasting greenery. A little later comes *Hamamelis mollis*, with its frost-proof yellow flowers. The herbaceous layer is occupied by bergenias, hellebores and pulmonarias, while the bulb layer is made up of snowdrops, crocuses and winter aconites and daffodils, with lesser spring bulbs – scillas and muscari (grape hyacinths) – in a supporting complementary role.

Hellebores form part of the garden's essential winter groups.

A foam of cherry blossom overhangs an early-flowering heather, a pastel spring combination.

The Spring Group

A fter the chill austerities of winter comes the glut of spring, which in this context lasts until the transition to earliest summer. It is pre-eminently the season of shrubs and flowering trees – the crab-apples, the cherries and the opulent magnolias. There are climbers too, especially the clematis. There are few perennials at this season, for their pattern of growth tends to preclude early flowering. The bulb season is continued by the Crown Imperials (*Fritillaria imperialis*), the tulips and the camassias.

The Summer Group

S ummer is predominantly the season of the perennials (the herbaceous layer) supported by repeat-flowering roses, fuchsias, shrubby potentillas, and the hydrangeas in all their diversity (the shrub layer). The bulb layer includes Paradise lilies (*Crinum powellii*), the nerines and Kaffir lilies

(*Schizostylis*), *Amaryllis belladonna* and the colchicums. Few trees are in flower at this season, though the catalpas excel, and rambling roses on trees flower at this time: the subtlely pink-toned, double 'Treasure Trove', the yellow-eyed 'Crimson Showers', the vigorous white 'Kiftsgate', 'Bobby James' and so on.

The Autumn Group

T he autumn spectrum is limited. On the one hand there are the mauves of the callicarpas (the shrub layer), both their leaves and their fruits, which can marry with pink and white colchicums and autumn crocus, the late-flowering, vivid magenta *Senecio pulcher*, the lilac-flowered *Hosta tardiflora* and the mauvy pinks of nerines and Kaffir lilies (*Schizostylis*), while on the other hand there are the reds, yellows and oranges of autumn colour, and berries, the tupelo (*Nyssa*), the acer, some of the cherries, the fruits of malus and sorbus, but little at ground level to tie in with them.

Colour Themes

The next step is to pick a colour theme for each season and then to work it out for each layer. Thus one might take a yellow and blue theme in early to mid-spring and an old roses and lavender theme (pink/mauve/purple) for mid to late summer, making the transition from spring to summer through a blue and white theme.

Spring (Early until Late).

Yellow is predominantly the colour of spring and its flowers. The bulb layer may be made up of the small early daffodils, 'Tête à Tête', 'Sprite', and the later ones mixed with the blues of *Scilla sibirica*, chionodoxa and the many hues of muscari. The perennial layer may be composed of the daisy flowers of golden doronicum (single or double), *Adonis vernalis* with

its clear yellow buttercup flowers or *A. amurensis* in shades of yellow or orange, the common wild primrose and its more sophisticated garden relatives, with the golden Crown Imperial (*Fritillaria imperialis* 'Maxima Lutea') whose emerging leaves are yellow at first, with the blues of forget-me-nots.

The shrub layer offers a glut of good things. On acid soils one can rely on rhodo-

ABOVE: Lily-flowering tulip 'White Triumphator'.

LEFT: A blue and yellow bed in late spring with Meconopsis cambrica, euphorbias, forget-me-nots and purple-blue aquilegias.

but 'Golden Ducat' has larger, pale yellow flowers.

There are no yellow trees this early, but Forsythia suspensa used as a climber will do duty, while many ceanothus may be used to provide the blue.

Transitions

In late spring one needs to make a transition from the colours of earlier spring to the colours of summer, though in very small gardens it simply may not be possible to include this element. The simplest way of making a transition from one group of colours to another is through whites, and this applies whether the transition is from one season to another or from one part of the garden to another.

The bulb layer can be made up of pheasant's eye narcissus (and its double form),

dendrons such as the violet-blue Rh. augustinii, 'Blue Tit', 'Blue Diamond', the pale yellow Rh. lutescens and 'Yellow Hammer' (for the whole art of using this outlandish tribe is to keep to a narrow palette). Subtler effects may be obtained with rosemaries and kerrias, in their many hues. The rosemary 'Primley Blue' is very free-flowering. Deeper hues are more tender. Kerria is normally egg-yolk yellow,

the snowflakes (Leucojum) and white tulips such as 'White Triumphator': the perennial layer with Dicentra spectabilis 'Alba', white aquilegias, white omphalodes, the white-variegated, white-flowered Lunaria annua, iberis and a white peony such as Paeonia emodi or P. obovata alba. The shrub layer offers a lot of good things at this season, Exochorda 'The Bride' being outstanding, Chaenomeles 'Nivalis', Choisya ternata, Drimys winteri, and the spiraeas, especially S. 'Arguta'. The tree layer may be made up of snowdrop trees (Halesia), fringe trees (Chionanthus) or various magnolias.

There are also at this season white-flowered climbers, of especial value where space is very limited, Clematis alpina 'White Moth', C. 'Burford White' and the white wisterias.

49

Hosta is one of the classic plants for contributing bold foliage, contrasted here with the feathery astilbe.

Colours of Summer

Against the neutral background of white the summer colours – pink/mauve/ purple, can begin to appear. The bulb layer has less to offer, the mauve-blue pyramids of *Scilla peruviana* to begin the season, the elegant alliums large and small, mostly in mauves and pinkish shades and also the pink Paradise lilies (*Crinum powellii*) coming much later. The herbaceous layer has much to offer: irises and peonies, oriental poppies and lupins, the hardy geraniums and nepeta, all blending very easily. The shrub layer is dominated by the old French roses, the Gallicas and Bourbons. The problem is their moment of glory is all too brief. The solution is to grow just one or two utterly ravishing old roses: the dark purplish Moss rose 'William Lobb' or the Gallica 'Président de Sèze', mauve-pink paling at its outer edges, the striped Bourbon 'Commandant de Beaurepaire' or 'Nuits de Young', a dusky maroon Moss; and then roses such as the pink 'Ballerina', lilac-pink 'Yesterday', the deep red white-eyed 'Marjorie Fair' or

the hybrid musk 'Mozart' with deep pink white-centered flowers to provide colour right through till the frosts, interspersed with casual campanulas, delphiniums, penstemons, and lavenders. The tree layer is best supplied by the violet *Abutilon* × *suntense*, with climbers such as the mauve *Solanum crispum* and later the various *Clematis patens* and *florida*, with the *C. viticella* cultivars providing a grand finale.

Foliage for all Seasons

For every plant that might be used in the garden one needs to consider not only the flower colour, and to which layer and which season of the scheme it belongs, but also its foliage, and its form, the overall shape or outline of the plant.

Foliage is important because it is there so much longer than the flowers, half the year for most plants, all the time for evergreens, so it is essential to consider what contribution the plant will make to the garden when not

The colours of summer: Geranium psilostemon and 'Johnson's Blue' lit up by the silver Stachys byzantina.

in flower. Some purists would claim that a wholly satisfying garden can be made of foliage alone.

One of the snares of small gardens is that most of the plants best suited to them have small leaves. A lot of small leaves do not make a good garden picture. The contrast of bold foliage is needed, the big, round leaves of bergenias, the hand-shaped leaves of *Fatsia japonica*. The classic plants for contributing bold foliage are acanthus, the Paradise lily (*Crinum*), agapanthus, whose leaves are strap-shaped, the heart-shaped leaves of hostas, *Melianthus major*, yuccas and phormiums, rodgersias, *Magnolia delavayi*, *M. grandiflora* or *M. macrophylla*, and some ferns, such as *Blechnum chilense*. Coppiced *Paulownia* may produce individual leaves nearly 3ft/1m across in the same season if it is pruned to the ground each spring.

51

Shape and Form

Just as important is the overall shape or form of the individual plants. A garden composed wholly of plants of humped or rounded outline will be as uninteresting as one composed wholly of plants with small leaves. Variety is the hallmark of good planting.

A few plants are so distinct that they are grown almost wholly for their shape or form – Irish yews for their uprightness, yuccas and phormiums for their sword-like leaves, acanthus for its architectural foliage – but most plants differ less markedly and this makes it all the more important to exploit these differences. Most hostas form mounds of leaves that overlap like an armadillo's scales, the counterpoint to which is a fern like *Dryopteris wallichiana*, shaped like a shuttle-cock. Lady's Mantle, *Alchemilla mollis*, creates the effect of foam, like the tide coming in, as its flowers tumble over its leaves, but gypsophila offers only a nebulous insubstantiality.

The essence is to combine plant shapes as carefully as one combines colours. Rounded shapes may be set upon a carpet of horizontal junipers, aubrieta or rock roses, or may be emphasized by groups of tall plants, spire-like foxgloves or delphiniums, wand-like verbascums. A few plants, like some campanulas, produce a carpet of leaves, and then bear their flowers on a crowd of upright stems, thus presenting quite different aspects in flower and out. Shrubs, trees and climbers extend the range of shapes available, as do the ferns and grasses, coming as they do from quite different sections of the plant world.

A match of horizontals and uprights: yews, topped by the wands of Deutzia monbeigii; alstroemerias make up the lower level.

All borders are graded: here background shrubs rise above alstroemerias, veronicas and lilies.

GRADING

Grading is the art of so arranging plants in a bed or border that it banks up from the front to the back. When well done it looks deceptively easy. The art is not only to know your plants, but to know how they will perform on your soil. Thus grading is something that one can usually only get approximately right first time.

When planning a graded border it is first necessary to envisage it in section, that is as a right-angle triangle whose base is the border, whose right-angle side is the wall or hedge behind the border and whose third side is an imaginary line drawn between the front of the border and the top of the wall, fence or

hedge. The next decision depends on the depth of the border: it is how many rows of planting there will be, for however cleverly one disguises it, borders are usually made up of low plants at the front, medium-sized plants in the middle and taller plants at the back. Sometimes there is only room for the foreground and middle ground, but in borders of 10ft/3m or more depth, four or five tiers may be possible.

In long borders the evenness of the grading needs to be interrupted by the occasional plant that is larger than the rest, and sometimes this larger plant may be the one to use to create the rhythm of the border. In general a steeply banked border will have more sense of depth and interest than a shallowly banked one. Taller plants will generally take up a larger ground area than smaller ones, and one needs deliberately to compensate for this.

Enhanced Perspectives

The Victorians were fond of false perspectives, the device whereby straight paths instead of having parallel sides, narrowed as they receded. Subtler effects can be achieved with foliage and colour.

If foliage is graded from largest in the foreground to smallest in the distance, then the smallest foliage will appear to be further away than it really is. The sequence of conifers, *Cephalotaxus harringtoniana* var. *drupacea*, yew (*Taxus baccata*) and Western hemlock (*Tsuga heterophylla*) would give such a graded sequence; or *Magnolia grandiflora*, followed by the holly *Ilex* × *altaclarensis* 'Camelliifolia, privet (*Ligustrum ovalifolium*) and *Lonicera nitida*, all of which could be clipped.

Colour can be used to reinforce the effect. If hot colours (yellow/orange/red) are used in the foreground, and misty colours, pale mauves and pinks, in the distance, this will appear to increase the distance between the two. The effect will be even greater if bright or dark green foliage is used in the foreground and grey foliage in the distance.

The effect is most dramatic if the foreground and distance are separated by a hedge or screen, so that the distant planting is seen through a gap or arch.

Plant form also plays its part. Upright shapes (pencil conifers), like any verticals tend to advance. Planted in the distance they will destroy the effect. They belong in the foreground. Rounded shapes and plants of imprecise form like some grasses belong in the distance.

ABOVE: *Terrace lit in early evening by ground-level lighting.*

OPPOSITE: *Hot colour in the foreground (crocosmia) and misty hues in the background stretch the distance.*

The Last Illusion

The lighting of a garden at night creates an effect more magical than anything else one can do. Entirely different effects will be created depending on whether the light source is seen or unseen. If seen, it is the light itself that is the attraction, whether a candle in a jam jar or a flaming torch. Such flickering lights draw the eye and give a garden limitless depth, where unfathomable forms and figures move furtively. Light from an unseen source is steadier, giving a sense of security: nonetheless it creates a world of its own, where the underneath of a leaf or branch is lit, rather than its upper surface. Such lights are best placed well below eye level and covered with a mushroom-like dome. Such lighting is particularly useful beside drives, paths and steps, making them safe to use at night. Terraces and sitting areas are often best lit from above, and lit as one might light a room, so that it is easy to read or eat by these lights.

A final type of lighting is that used underwater, in pools and ponds. At night the water magnifies the light, and fountains become cascades of molten brilliance.

lovers wilt in dry conditions. It also helps to see how the problem is solved in the natural world. Beech woods, for example, make their own rain shadow, and cast very dense shade. Four tiers of vegetation have evolved to co-exist here. The tallest are the trees, which create the canopy and rain shadow. Below them is an understorey of trees and climbers, hollies, hazels and yew, for example, with honeysuckle and wild clematis. Below this is a layer of essentially herbaceous plants, geraniums and wood-ruff, several umbellifers, sedges and grasses as well as ferns, whose fronds have evolved to exploit just such conditions. Finally there is a carpet of bulbs whose life-cycle interlocks with that of the trees – snowdrops, bluebells, and little wind-flowers. These put on their greenery and grow in winter when the trees are bare, and cope with the summer dryness by going dormant.

Rain shadows in the garden need to be dealt with in a similar way, but it is also necessary to adjust one's mental horizons. It is no good expecting the excitement of an herbaceous border in a rain shadow. One has to seek a quieter, more appropriate idiom, relying more on contrasts of foliage than flower.

RAIN SHADOWS

Rain shadows occur where the path of the prevailing wind is blocked by a building or by trees, casting a shadow where no rain falls. Such areas are usually also heavily shaded, creating a double difficulty since far fewer plants will grow in shade than in sun, and fewer still in dry shade.

In considering how to deal with such an area it is worth remembering that the most satisfactory gardens are made by fitting the right plants to the right places. Sun-lovers languish in shade, moisture-

Naturalized Anemone appenina *form part of the bulb layer.*

The Shrub Layer

If the trees casting the rain shadow are in one's own garden, then sometimes a pleasing contrast of verticals and horizontals can be made by leaving the trees with bare trunks and planting a carpet beneath them; but more usually a shrub layer is needed to fill the void between the canopy and the ground.

The most drought-tolerant of all shade-bearing shrubs is *Ruscus aculeatus*, a bushy plant with matt green stems and fans of deep green, spine-tipped leaves. Females bear showy red berries in winter, but there must be a male nearby. More attractive is *R. hypoglossum* with arching stems and glossy broad leaves. Almost as tolerant is the Oregon grape, *Mahonia aquifolium*, whose evergreen leaves turn purplish in winter. It bears blue-black berries and produces fragrant yellow flowers at the end of winter.

Skimmias and aucubas provide good, rounded shrubs for dry shade. The skimmias have narrowly oval evergreen leaves, bear fragrant greenish-white flowers in spring, and the females bear red berries in winter, if planted four females to one male. *Skimmia japonica* is a strong grower. *Aucuba japonica* is best in its narrow-leafed forms, *A. j.* 'Salicifolia' which is female and bears big red berries, and *A. j.* 'Lance Leaf' which is the necessary male.

Where variegation is needed *Euonymus fortunei* forms are ideal. *E. f.* 'Emerald 'n' Gold' is dark green with lime-green variegation if grown in shade (gold in full sun) while *E. f.* 'Silver Queen' is white-variegated in shade (cream in full sun).

The Bulb Layer

The ground surface may be varied with a pattern of stone or slabs, and pebbles or pea-grit, or simply bricks laid in herringbone or basket-weave. If the surface becomes slippery scrub it with a mild bleach solution. Then consider the bulb layer. The season may start at the turn of the year with *Cyclamen*

The shield fern, Polystichum setiferum, will tolerate dry shade; this is a very finely cut form.

coum in pink and white, to be followed by early snowdrops in one area, and late snowdrops in another. Most crocuses will not open their flowers unless sunlight falls directly on them, so may not be worthwhile. Early daffodils come next, then mid-season daffodils and the later narcissus. The smaller-flowered ones seem most appropriate here. Overlapping these are sky-blue scillas and grape hyacinths, and chionodoxa, to be followed if one likes them by bluebells (but these can take over entirely). Overlapping these are the windflowers, *Anemone nemorosa*, *A. apennina* and *A. blanda*, in blue, white or pink, and the garden primroses in white, pink, red or shades of yellow,

the intense blues of *Ompha-lodes cappadocica*, and the showy white of Lady's Smock, overlapped by the arching wands of Solomon's seal. But once the trees come into leaf all these die down, leaving bare earth.

Continuity of Interest

Some continuity of flower can be achieved with early and late honeysuckles, and by growing roses and clematis up through the trees, though these will only flower where their heads emerge into the sun, underplanted with *Geranium nodosum*, whose flowers may be deep or pale mauve, in bold drifts.

Continuity of interest must

rely on the play of light and shade on plants of contrasting form: finely dissected ferns with the round bulk of *Skimmia japonica* or the fragrant-leafed S. *anquetilia*, tiny leafed boxwood plants contrasted with the bold leaves of aspidistras. There are many forms of box, some with tinier or variegated leaves. The epimediums, with their dainty pink, white or yellow flowers, have elegant leaves, often flushed pink in spring. The male fern, *Dryopteris filix-mas*, will do well in dry shade, as will the false male fern, *D. pseudo-mas*: both have fine garden forms with crests or other variants. The shield ferns, *Polystichum*, which are very finely dissected, will all enjoy these conditions, as will all the polypodiums. Evergreen perennials to give form to the ground surface are *Galax urceolata*, with its big round leaves and wands of dainty white flowers, the variegated or the rather rare white-fruited form of *Iris foetidissima* called 'Fructu Albo', and the woodrush, *Luzula sylvatica*. The lilyturfs, *Ophiopogon japonicus* and *O. intermedius* create a grass-like effect, but grow too dense for bulbs to come up through them.

The Radical Alternative

There is, however, a radical alternative. One can lay seep-hoses, thereby resolving the problem of dryness. Shade on its own is far less of a problem. On acid soils, in well irrigated shade, camellias will flourish, and rhododendrons, which include the dwarf, so-called evergreen azaleas and the scented deciduous azaleas, while on alkaline soils the viburnums and lilacs come into their own. At mid-summer the hydrangeas come into flower and stay colourful till autumn: the mop-heads wilt sooner if dry than any other plant.

The season could begin with the same bulbs as in the unirrigated area, with the addition of the pulmonarias, many of which have grey or marbled leaves, and the bergenias with their large, nearly round leaves and big heads of pink or white flowers. These can be

Camellia 'Galaxie' thrives on acid soil which is moist and humus-rich.

followed by a planting of hostas, in green, blue or white-variegated forms, with ferns such as *Adiantum pedatum japonicum* or *Dryopteris erythrosora*, both of whose new fronds are pink in spring; with foxgloves and thalictrum, especially T. 'Hewitt's Double', with tiny mauve pompon flowers which tone perfectly, pink or white Martagon lilies, and the geraniums 'Johnson's

Blue' and pink *G. endressii*. The season could carry on with the pink-flowered, bronze-leafed *Begonia evansiana* and conclude with the stumpy, deep mauve flowers of *Hosta tardiflora* and the white flowers of *Saxifraga fortunei* with green or brown leaves beside the mauve spires of *Liriope muscari*, the pale *L.m.* 'Superba' and the dark 'Royal Purple', and the autumn cyclamen.

WILD CORNERS

Control is the essence of gardening. So it is always a delight to have a part of the garden where less control is exercised. A wild area demands the very least control. But wild gardens are still gardens. They do not come into being by doing nothing. There is an intention behind them. And part of the joy is that the wildness seems wilder by contrast with the manicured area, and that too gains by the contrast. The ambience of a wild area is muted, offering an almost careless rapture.

Even in a quite small garden it is possible to have a wild area. If the garden is big enough to divide in two, then the area near the house will be the orderly one, the farther compartment the wild one. In even smaller gardens a mown area may separate the terrace and its flowers from the wild reaches of the garden. Or it may just be an island bed of wildness set in a neat lawn.

At its simplest a wild area may just be rough grass and spring bulbs, cut down to 4in/10cm once their leaves are gone and then rough-mown three or four times. Or it may be a tapestry of seemingly wild flowers. Start with a medlar (or a hawthorn, hazel or wild apple) and then carpet the ground with primroses and violets, daisies and periwinkle, forget-me-nots and gilly flowers (*Matthiola perennis*), chamomile and columbines, cow-parsleys and a few wild strawberries. Such a planting, once established, will flourish unattended: only the grass needs cutting, three or four times a year.

In more shaded gardens a more woodland effect is needed. Start the season with snowdrops and windflowers, golden winter aconites (*Eranthis hyemalis*), and the lime-green flowers of *Helleborus foetidus*. Continue with ground-covering pulmonarias and hardy geraniums, using the arching wands of Solomon's seal and the stout nankeen heads of euphorbias to give height. After these come daffodils and oriental hellebores, followed by Queen Anne's lace and then the foxgloves, erupting from a sea of geraniums – magenta G. *sanguineum*, dark purple G. *phaeum* or blue G. *sylvaticum* overlapping the astilbes and the Turk's cap lilies, *L. martagon*.

A totally different idiom of wildness may be created using ornamental grass with bergenia, acanthus and spiraeas, liriope, sedum, rudbeckia and caryopteris. The essential grasses are *Pennisetum alopecuroides*, *Panicum virgatum* 'Rehbraun' and *Calamagrostis acutiflora* 'Stricta' which all look well together: tall *Miscanthus sinensis* or the elegant *Molinia arundinacea* 'Windspiel', which almost dances in the breeze. These should be cut to the ground in late spring.

A more exotic kind of wildness can be created with a few bamboos, a fern or two, and some grass-like plants. *Phyllostachys bambusoides* is an archetypal bamboo, with tall, well spaced canes and delicate leafage. P. *aurea* has knobbly close-set canes. Underplant with *Fatsia japonica*, some hardy palms, a few aspidistra and some dramatic ferns, such as *Dryopteris wallichiana*, all set in a ground cover of *Ophiopogon japonicus*.

RIGHT: The evergreen *Helleborus foetidus will seed itself freely, though it is too useful to be a nuisance. Its ice-green bells, rimmed with maroon, are long-lasting from late winter and throughout spring.*

BELOW: *Erythroniums and the white form of* Fritillaria meleagris *in grass. Both bulbs enjoy moist soil.*

INDEX

Roger Grounds is a garden designer, horticultural writer and lecturer. His publications include both reference works on grasses and ferns as well as books on design, including his recent The White Garden jointly written by Diana Grenfell, with whom he has made a formal colour-themed garden at Apple Court, Lymington, Hampshire in the South of England. They have four National Reference Collections of plants and a nursery specializing in hostas, hemerocallis and unusual plants.

ISBN 1-55859-661-5